D0430445

Say Chic

A Collection of French
Words We Can't Live Without

FRANÇOISE BLANCHARD
and
JEREMY LEVEN

Scribner

NEW YORK   LONDON   TORONTO   SYDNEY

SCRIBNER
A Division of Simon & Schuster, Inc.
1230 Avenue of the Americas
New York, NY 10020

First Scribner trade paperback edition July 2007
Originally published in France in 2004 by Les Editions Diateino
Published by arrangement with Les Editions Diateino

SCRIBNER and design are trademarks of
Macmillan Library Reference USA, Inc., used under license
by Simon & Schuster, the publisher of this work.

For information about special discounts for bulk purchases,
please contact Simon & Schuster Special Sales:
1-800-456-6798 or business@simonandschuster.com

Designed by Kyoko Watanabe
Text set in Charlotte

Manufactured in the United States of America

1   3   5   7   9   10   8   6   4   2

Library of Congress Control Number: 2006039165

ISBN-13: 978-1-4165-6184-2
ISBN-10: 1-4165-6184-6

Say Chic

Foreword

IT HAS BECOME obvious to us that the English language is incorporating French vocabulary at an ever-increasing speed, and that, as it does so, some words are retaining their original French meanings, and some are not. Others have taken on totally new meanings and then been returned to France, where they have completely replaced the words from which they were derived, in an impressive display of foreign exchange.

Accordingly, we thought it might be interesting to track down some of this semantic ebb and flow. What French words are now common

Foreword

English (such as *café* and *chauffeur*), what words have changed their meanings entirely (such as *au pair*), what did the words mean originally, and how did the French get them? We arrived at a list of about 120 French words and expressions that have become part of our everyday English vocabulary, and were quite pleased with our work until we discovered that we had merely touched the tip of a vast iceberg. Indeed, our list soon reached more than 400 words and was still growing. Some were very common expressions, while others were more obscure, and still others had deeply mysterious circumstances surrounding their "adoption" by the English language.

Since this book was never intended to be an exhaustive dictionary, we decided to focus on the French words most frequently in use in ordinary English-language conversation. This reduced our selection to 70 or so words which we believed to be relatively common, although, from to time to time, we found ourselves choosing words less because of their common usage than because they surprised or amused us—an author's prerogative.

In most, but not all, cases, we first define the word as used in French, then describe its origin and derivation. Then (when we can determine it) we relate how the word found its way into the English language, what its current English meaning has become, and, finally, whether, if the meaning has changed, the new English meaning has been reincorporated into French.

We have retained the French spelling whenever we can, while listing all other possible forms (whether correct or not) one might encounter. As for the delicate matter of pronunciation, we have chosen not to use phonetic symbols and opted for a more mnemotechnic (from the French *mnémotechnique*) method. When the pronunciation differs from French to English, we make sure to specify both the English and French ways to pronounce the word (in that order), so the reader may play his linguistic cards in whatever way he believes will most impress friends, family, and associates on both sides of the Atlantic and the English Channel, thereby displaying both his *savoir faire* and his *panache*.

Au naturel

[oh nah cha *rel* / oh nah tyoo *rel*]

Americans have adopted this expression to describe things accomplished in a natural manner. And for those who consider nothing to be more "natural" than nudity, the term is also used as a synonym for "naked," a reference to Eden's occupants going about their business in their birthday suits.

For the French, this expression also signifies things not prepared or seasoned. A can of tuna will be labelled *au naturel* to indicate that the fish is soaking in its own seawater rather than oil or tomato sauce. An additional meaning in French refers to the "real-lifeness" of something or someone, as opposed to its representation. In considering a photograph of an exceptionally attractive woman, one might ask whether she looks as astonishingly beautiful *au naturel*, that is, in real life. This distinction between the English and French usage is especially important to remember when referring to the image of a friend's wife, whom one might, indeed, be interested in seeing *au naturel*.

Au pair

[oh *pear*]

Used in both French and English, the expression *au pair* describes a young foreigner who is responsible for child care (and occasionally light housework) in exchange for room and board. More generally, *au pair* indicates an arrangement whereby people exchange services without making monetary payments.

The current French meaning for *pair* refers to someone equal in value (as in the English word "par") or with the same social standing and background, and, indeed, the word originally expressed the notion of parity, especially regarding the exchange rate of a currency. Then in the mid-1800s, wealthy families began to hire private *au pairs* (tutors) to teach their children in exchange for board and lodging, until, today, the young *au pair* has replaced the tutor in the home and now is responsible for child care.

The expression has travelled around the world, much like the young working men and women it describes, since it was first borrowed from the French by the Americans, who then were kind enough to return it to France with its current meaning.

Bête noire

[bet nwar]

Literally translated as "black beast," this refers to something or someone especially hated or feared. It also applies to a recurring obstacle in one's life which can be neither avoided nor overcome. Since beasts tend to be, in themselves, something to be feared, regardless of their hue, one might wonder why this particular beast must be black. One can only surmise that one might be less apt to flee from, say, a dreaded yellow or pink beast.

Bidet

[bee *day*]

The *bidet* is a basin specially designed to accommodate the bathing of one's private parts, especially those of the female. The word was first recorded in English back in 1630 and has kept its original usage ever since. In French, *bidet* comes from the old verb *bider* ("to trot") and is also the name of a small ponylike horse, ridden in the crouching position with one's legs drawn up to avoid dragging them on the ground. No more need be said of the origin.

Boutique

[boo *teek*]

First recorded in France during the fourteenth century, the word *boutique* used to be *botica*, which itself came from the Greek *apothêkê* and referred to small retail shops selling various merchandise, from food to shoes. The English, upon borrowing the word in the mid-1900s, applied it to stores selling fancy women's clothes and jewelry, following the trend set by Parisian couturiers who had begun opening small specialty shops selling exclusive fashionable accessories.

In the seventeenth century, *boutique* acquired another meaning in France and came to be used as a metaphor for men's and women's sexual organs, in the sense of being merchandise available for purchase. This particular definition has largely disappeared, so one need not be overly concerned when a *boutique* owner

greets a customer with a cheery, "Look what I have in store for you!"

Brunette

[brew *net*]

Used in English to describe a woman with brown hair or eyes or a dark complexion, *brunette* is the feminine version of *brun* ("brown"), most often used when talking about hair. The French added the suffix *-ette*, an expression of endearment, conveying a sense of cuteness and smallness. The literal translation would then have to be "a short, cute brown-haired girl," but the French don't use it that way—in fact, they don't use it at all, although, from time to time, cute little blonde girls are called *blondinettes*. The reader should beware, however, of calling a redhead a *roussette* (even though a redhead in French is, indeed, a *rousse*), since that would amount to calling her a dogfish, tropical bat, or edible frog.

Cabaret

[kab uh *ray*]

The origin of *cabaret* goes back to the thirteenth-century Netherlands, with the word *cabret,* and to the Picardie region (located north of Paris), with the word *camberete,* taken from the local dialect, which translates as "small room." *Cabaret* was once a synonym for *bistro,* a tavern or small bar that served alcohol and coffee. At the end of the seventeenth century, a different meaning of the word was recorded when *cabaret* was also used to designate a small piece of furniture that served as what we call today a minibar.

Later on, it took the current meaning: a nightclub that provides clients with musical and dancing performances, as well as food and drinks. The most famous Parisian *cabarets* are the Moulin Rouge, the Crazy Horse, and the Lido, which feature topless dancers adorned in glitter and feathers, obligatory for all French *cabarets,* but, sadly, a tradition that seems never to have crossed the English Channel or the Atlantic to the same delightful extent.

Canard

[kah *nard*]

A *canard* is a "small wild or domesticated web-footed broad-billed swimming bird usually having a depressed body and short legs." But there is more to this duck than meets the eye. Indeed, in English, when identifying something as a *canard* you'll be referring to a deliberately misleading story fabricated to make a fool out of someone. This usage derives from the French expression *bailler un canard à moitié,* meaning literally "to sell half a duck." We can thank the Emperor Napoleon for this, as his Grand Army used to publish a newsletter of imperial propaganda to keep the public informed of its numerous victories abroad. Since the front page of the paper conspicuously displayed the imperial eagle, the emperor's symbol, those readers who did not take kindly to the paper challenging their credulity soon renamed it *Le canard impérial* ("The Imperial Duck"). In 1848, the *Canard* was a small newspaper published occasionally to report scandalous news, such as a particularly hideous crime. Its content was never taken especially seriously, as it spread many false stories, or *canards,* embellished in the grand tradition of the emperor.

When the well-known French newspaper *Le Canard Enchaîné* (literally "The Chained Duck") was created in 1915, its purpose was to fight the propaganda and censorship perpe-

trated by the government during the First World War.
To achieve this at once
admirable and daunting
task, the *Canard* chose to
convey information with a
satirical and ironic humor as
a dare to censorship. To
this day, this *Canard* has
done well enough to avoid selling advertise-
ments within its pages in order to stay afloat.
Where this *Canard* is concerned, everything
has been just ducky.

Françoise Blanchard *and* Jeremy Leven

Cause célèbre

[cohz seh *lebr*]

The adjective *célèbre* means "famous" or "celebrated," while the French word *cause* has numerous definitions, such as "origin," "reason," "principle," and especially "lawsuit." Indeed, notable legal cases and trials that drew a lot of public attention have been called *causes célèbres* since the twelfth century in France, and since the mid-eighteenth century in England. Today the phrase applies to people, episodes, or notorious incidents that attract widespread interest. *Cause célèbre* and "celebrity" share the same etymology, which may account for why the two intermingle so easily, blending inevitably into a popular feature of modern life, the scandal.

C'est la vie!

[say la vee]

As is widely known, *"c'est"* is a contraction of *"ceci/cela est"* ("this/that is"). Literally translated as "that's life," *c'est la vie* is an expression that can be used in French in either a literal or a figurative way, to stress the fact that someone or something represents life (for example, in a slogan such as *"l'eau, c'est la vie,"* "water is life"), or to express one's acknowledgment of an undeniable fact. The English borrowed the expression and its metaphorical sense to express the inevitability of what happens in the "real" world, as opposed to the ideal world, which we would prefer. Over time the phrase has been applied primarily to things going poorly, as, for example, when Paris is hit with still another metro strike in the middle of rush hour. *C'est la vie.*

C'est magnifique!

[say mah nyee *feek*]

This French expression meaning "It's marvelous!" owes its fame to Pierre Jean-François Joseph Bosquet (1810–1861), Marshal of France, who took part in the Algerian conquest and distinguished himself during the Crimean War. In 1854, he was overheard commenting on the unfortunate charge of the Light Brigade at Balaklava and supposedly said, *"C'est mag-*

nifique, mais ce n'est pas la guerre." ("It's magnif-icent, but it isn't war.")

The French are as fond of this expression as they are of the event or object it describes, and tend to utilize the phrase on every possible occasion.

Chaise lounge

[shayz lounge / shayz long]

First recorded in the late eighteenth century in English, *chaise lounge* seems to have derived from a spelling mistake when it was borrowed from the French, who actually spell it *chaise longue* (literally "long chair"). The piece of furniture it describes is, however, the same reclining chair used for resting and "lounging" that can often be found around swimming pools or decks, though one would be hard-pressed to find such a *chaise* in a lounge.

The French also use *transat* (short for *transatlantique,* "transatlantic," in reference to deck chairs on ocean liners) as a synonym for *chaise longue,* which they also turned into the expression *faire de la chaise longue* ("to do some *chaise longue*"), meaning to rest on such a chair, however bizarre it may sound in English.

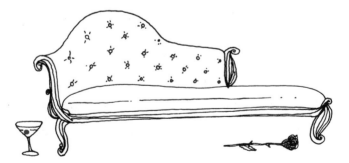

Charlatan

[*shar* luh tan / *shar* la tonh]

From the Italian *ciarlatano,* which itself comes from the verb *ciarlare,* meaning "to speak pompously," *charlatan* has been used in French since the sixteenth century to identify salesmen who would travel from town to town selling medical remedies at local marketplaces and fairs. Later on, it was used to describe the fake healers and doctors who pretended to possess marvelous curative secrets.

Upon its arrival into the English language, back in the early seventeenth century, *charlatan* kept its original meaning and is now used by both French and English to mean any kind of impostor attempting to deceive others with unwarrantable promises and pretensions.

The origin of the word remains as dubious as the speeches churned out by those it describes. Some sources refer to the town of Cerreto, located in Italy, near Spoleto, where miraculous potions were manufactured, then to be sold across the marketplaces of Europe. The inhabitants of Cerreto, who were called *cerretanos*, may have bragged too much about their local remedies, and the ignominy has stuck.

Chauffeur

[*show* fur / show *fur*]

From the French verb *chauffer* ("to heat"), *chauffeur* literally translates as "stoker," referring to a person responsible for maintaining a fire or boiler. Back in the 1800s, a *chauffeur* was also a kind of robber who would burn the feet of his victims to extort money. Fortunately, the contemporary *chauffeur*'s responsibilities are limited to operating a vehicle. While English-speakers apply the term specifically to one who is paid to drive a client around in a pri-

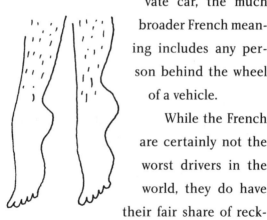

vate car, the much broader French meaning includes any person behind the wheel of a vehicle.

While the French are certainly not the worst drivers in the world, they do have their fair share of reckless drivers and road hogs, called *chauffards,* an insulting term that depicts them as sub-stantially less competent drivers than regular *chauffeurs*. When called this to their faces, the are known to become overheated.

Chauvinism

[*show* vih nism]

Nicolas Chauvin, a loyal and enthusiastic soldier in Napoleon's Grand Army, was wounded several times at various battles during the emperor's reign. After the exile of the Little Corporal, Chauvin remained devoted to his emperor, despite the ridiculously small pension to which he was entitled in return for loyal services rendered to the French Empire. His notorious naïve patriotism earned him the misfortune of becoming a recurrent character in several vaudevilles, such as *La Cocarde Tricol-ore* by Cogniard, in which his persona would proudly shout out boastful *"cocoricos"* (cock-a-doodle-doos, the Gallic rooster being the sym-bol of France).

Soon after, *chauvin* entered the French lan-guage as an adjective to describe an overzeal-ous patriot blinded by his fanatical devotion to his country. The question that remains unan-swered is, of course, whether the French were chauvinistic before Chauvin came along or whether he simply personified a tendency.

Françoise Blanchard *and* Jeremy Leven

Cherchez la femme

[share shay la *fahm*]

Literally "look for the woman," specifically the woman who is responsible for whatever problem the man is encountering, the expression has historically been used during police investigations when looking for the most likely motive of a Frenchman for some heinous act. Sources give Alexandre Dumas (1802–1870) credit for the expression, while others mention Joseph Fouché (1759–1820), a political figure during the French Revolution. While the expression *"cherchez l'homme"* does not exist, many Frenchwomen have spent a not inconsiderable amount of their time searching for men who do not attribute every deficiency and misfortune to *la femme*. There are reportedly Frenchwomen who claim to be equally responsible for a man's happiness as for his misfortune.

And this brings us to the second meaning of *cherchez la femme* in France, which refers simply to the quest for a female partner, especially, as the article *la* specifies, the "one" woman. Anecdotal evidence indicates that Frenchmen and Frenchwomen are no more successful at this than their English-speaking counterparts.

Françoise Blanchard *and* Jeremy Leven

Chic

[sheek]

Apart from being the French word for "elegant," *chic* is also the fashionable way to describe someone or something sophisticated, charming, or stylish—much the way the reader of this little tome might seem to be in subsequent conversation! We all hope to become, as the French would say, very *B.C.B.G.* (short for *bon chic, bon genre*), literally meaning "good style, good type," initials used to describe someone whose appearance is both classy and in exceptionally good taste.

The origin of the word goes back to the late eighteenth century, when the French used it in reference to one's ability to paint without a model, only imagining the object to be depicted on canvas. Thus, "to paint *de chic*" implied that the painting was done entirely from one's imagination. Later on, the noun applied to one's know-how and ability. In fact,

the expression *avoir le chic pour* translates as "to have a knack for" and refers to a person's talent for something, a phrase not to be confused with *avoir du chic* ("to have some chic"), which means that an individual (and, sometimes, a thing) possesses elegance and ease.

Used in a more familiar way, the adjective *chic* can also be a synonym for "nice" when talking about an individual, event, or gesture. As the English adopted yet another word of their Gallic neighbors', the French may have thought it *chic* to return the favor by borrowing the English adjective *smart* as a synonym for their own *chic*. What the English now call *très chic*, the French now describe as *très smart*. And how smart is that?

Cinéma vérité

[*see* nay mah *vay* ree tay]

The concept of "truth cinema" (the literal translation of *cinéma vérité,* which, itself, was translated by Jean Rouch from the Russian *Kino Pravda*) goes back to a 1919 manifesto by Russian filmmaker Dziga Vertov (1895–1954). However, technology being what it is, *cinéma vérité* had to wait for the 1960s for its concept to prosper.

Unlike the ambitions of most Hollywood productions, *cinéma vérité* filmmakers focused on realism, filming ordinary people in their own homes or surroundings, using handheld cameras. Dialogue was neither written nor rehearsed, nor were actors involved, props or sets used, or big budgets needed. The unobtrusive cameras and crew were so discreet that they were able truly to explore the intimacy of people's lives, recording nothing but real and sincere conversations and emotions, much as in documentary filmmaking. The editing room was where the story came together.

Among the big names that mark the history of *cinéma vérité* are Jean Rouch (1917–2004), Michel Brault (b. 1928), Richard Leacock (b. 1921), Albert Maysles (b. 1926), Fred Wiseman (b. 1930), and Karel Reisz (1926–2002). *Cinéma vérité* has come and gone and now come again, its latest incarnation being "reality TV," much to the dismay, one suspects, of all the artists above.

Cliché

[klee *shay*]

The word *cliché* comes from the eighteenth-century verb *clicher,* which referred to the technique, used mostly in printing, of pouring melted metal into a shaped mold. The verb itself is onomatopoeia for the sound of the die falling upon the cast iron. The first definition of *cliché* applied to the embossed plaque used in the printing process to reproduce numerous copies of a page.

In the mid-1900s, the word *cliché* was granted a new usage in photography, referring to the negative image of a picture, from which many copies can be made, and has ever since been commonly used in French as a synonym for photograph.

As with the printing *cliché*, which processed thousands of copies, the word *cliché* came to apply to worn-out expressions that have been used thousands of times before, never changing, becoming hackneyed, dull, trivial banalities. *Cliché* as an adjective describes a stereotyped and worn-out situation, plot, expression, or idea. As communication proliferates because of the Internet, finding something—anything—that is not a *cliché* has become increasingly challenging.

Coquette

[koh *ket*]

Coquette is the feminine of *coquet* (literally "little rooster"), used to describe a dandy, in the case of a man, or a woman so eager to seduce others that she struts around as a barnyard cock might among the hens. Faithful to her

reputation as a vain and trifling woman, she puts a great deal of thought and effort into her looks and adores being the center of attention in her exploitation of men.

In the seventeenth century, a theater actress who played the part of a beautiful and elegant woman was said to play the part of a *grande coquette.* The word took on many meanings over the years, such as "cozy" when talking about a home, or "nice" when referring to a rather impressive amount of money. But the most memorable usage of the word in French has been as a name for the male organ, in recognition, we suppose, of its frequent longing for attention.

Coup de grâce

[koo duh *grahs* / koo duh *grass*]

Utilized in French and English since the end of the 1700s, the first meaning of this expression, which literally translates as "blow of mercy," applied to a fatal blow that put a merciful ending to an individual's suffering, especially after an execution, in the event that the squad of marksmen had an "off day." That placing a loaded gun against someone's skull and pulling the trigger should be considered an act of "grace" is, at best, somewhat paradoxical.

Thankfully, a more figurative usage has developed, and the phrase *coup de grâce* can now refer to any action or event that puts an end to something—such as a career or reputation—with the same undeniable finality as a bullet to the head.

Debonair

[deb uh *nair*]

From the French *débonnaire* (itself composed of the three words *de, bonne,* and *aire,* meaning "from noble origins"), the expression comes from the eagle's nest, which was called an *aire* in the early eleventh century. The bird, of such magnificent stature, demonstrated great dignity and pride, just as their lineage would inspire knights to respectfully honor their ancestors by proving their bravery in tournaments and duels, or by enrolling in Crusades.

In error, the original phrase was replaced with *de bon air,* referring to the friendly looks of an individual. Thus, the meaning of the word evolved to describe someone graceful, affable, courteous, and gentle. In French, a charming and sophisticated man may be called *debonair,* as may anyone looking cheerful, carefree, and optimistic.

But, in French, *debonair* often implies another characteristic—weakness. In fact, a husband who is overly accommodating of his wife's adultery, mostly out of frailty and foolish leniency, is called *debonair.* One suspects that the valiant Crusaders would not have been pleased.

Françoise Blanchard *and* Jeremy Leven

Début

[*day* byoo / day *byoo*]

In French, since the seventeenth century, *début* ("beginning"), as opposed to *but* ("end" or "goal"), was used to describe the opening move in a game, and the verb *débuter* (from the sixteenth century) then meant "to make one's first move." Recorded in English in 1752, the word, which at first applied to any start or commencement, acquired a new meaning and came to signify one's formal introduction into society. A young lady who first appeared at an official social function was thus called a *débutante*. In fact, the *débutantes'* ball is a tradition that lives on, and it is with this modern significance that *débutante* came back to French, which had been using the word simply to describe any kind of beginner or novice. The abbreviation of *débutantes* ("debs") is also used in both languages, though its paternity belongs to the English.

First used as a noun in expressions such as "to make one's *début*" (in reference to one's first public, screen, or theatrical appearance), in English *début* turned into a verb ("to début"), which is now used as a synonym for presenting or introducing oneself for the first time to the public. In today's world of short memory spans, for the celebrity a smashing *début* may quickly become *le but*.

The French have carried all this one stop further, introducing the phrase *faux débutant,* which describes an individual who is not, in fact, a beginner but "modestly" claims to be a novice, taking easy beginning French classes where he can excel and impress all present, or inducing one who has just learned to Roller-blade to accompany him and then spinning in circles down the pavement on one skate.

Décolleté

[day kohl *tay* / day koh leh *tay*]

From the verb *décolleter,* which means "to bare (a woman's) neck and shoulders," *décolleté* is used when describing a low-necked dress or gown. *Décolleté* arrived in English in the early nineteenth century intact from the French in both form and meaning. Its origin lies in the word *collet*, a French noun that designates the part of clothing that encircles the neck. As dresses (and morals) evolved, the *collet* plunged, leaving the neck uncovered, thus creating a *décolleté*.

Another word sprang from *collet*: *décolletage*, which points to the upper part of a *décolleté* dress, or the cleavage exposed by such a descending bodice. The attentive observer may have noticed that today dresses have been doing substantially more than just baring the neck and shoulders. "De-navelage" appears to be rising as rapidly as *décolletage* is descending, leaving little in between.

Demimondaine

[de mee mon *dain* /
de mee *mon* dain]

Written *demi-mondaine* in French, this expression translates literally as "half-socialite" and designates a woman of the *demimonde* (half-world or netherworld), in other words, a courtesan. Indeed, *mondaine,* from the ecclesiastic Latin *mundanus,* refers to the worldly nature of things, as opposed to what is holy and sacred. *Demimonde* thus applies to the class that includes women of the underworld, who are characterized by questionable reputations, promiscuous behaviors, and, most importantly, wealthy clients. In comparison, high-class society is often called *beau monde* ("beautiful world" or "beautiful people") or *haute société* ("high society").

These *demimondaines,* however, were not mere prostitutes. They proliferated from the mid-1700s into the *belle époque,* which ended with World War I. Thanks to their aristocratic and extravagant lovers, some of them managed to gain influential positions and high social status, as well as considerable wealth. Women such as the Comtesse du Barry (1743–1793), Madame de Pompadour (1721–1764), Lina Cavalieri (1874–1944), Hortense Schneider (1833–1920), Caroline (la Belle) Otero (1868–1965), and many others whose names have survived the test of time are a tribute to their great influence in society. Their involvement in politics and the arts can't be denied, and they have played a significant role in France's cultural history.

Today, however, with the golden age of *demimondaines* sadly behind us, the expression *demimonde* now applies to a group of people engaged in illegal activities or characterized by a lack of success, in other words, a pack of losers operating on the sordid fringes of society. How sad for those who understood that being disreputable does not necessarily mean a loss of class.

Discothèque

[dis co *tek* / *dis* co tek]

This contemporary word was first recorded in French in the early twentieth century to designate a collection of phonograph records, as well as the piece of furniture designed to shelter such a collection. In the early 1960s, one could borrow records from a public *discothèque* in France, which operated much like a public library. In fact, the French word for "library" *(bibliothèque)* is made of two Greek words: *biblion* for "book," and *thêkê* for "case" or "warehouse." The word *discothèque* was created based on this pattern.

It wasn't long until recordings on vinyl disks made their way into nightclubs. Renamed *discothèques,* these dance halls played recorded popular music characterized by a fast tempo and Latino percussions. The abbreviation *(disco)* is commonly used today when mentioning such popular dance halls. For reasons known only to the French, in France *dis-cothèques* are now called *boîtes* ("boxes").

Double entendre

[double aun *tandr* /
dooble aun *tandr*]

What an odd coincidence that a mistranslation should be the origin of an expression that points out the ambiguity of a phrase that can be interpreted in more than one way. Indeed, the actual (and correct) French equivalent is the expression *double entente,* which is composed of the words *double* ("double" or "twice") and *entente* ("comprehension"), referring to a double meaning.

The English adopted the term during the seventeenth century and replaced *entente* with *entendre*, a French verb that means "to hear." Among the many interpretations of a *double entendre* is often one suggestive of indecency. The French are quite fond of these word games and, although Britney Spears' French counterpart, Alizée, may play the goody-two-shoes role, a double listen to the lyrics of her songs will reveal a fair number of *double entendres.*

Françoise Blanchard *and* Jeremy Leven

Éminence grise

[ay mee nonce *greez*]

Louis XIII (1601–1643) may have officially ruled over France for thirty-three years, but the real powers behind the throne were the politically ambitious Cardinal de Richelieu (born Armand Jean du Plessis, 1585–1638) and Père Joseph (born François Joseph Leclerc du Tremblay, 1577–1638), a fervent Capuchin determined to rid France of all heretics, who was Richelieu's confidant and personal secretary.

Their strong influence over the king produced an almost endless cadre of jealous rivals who would call Richelieu and du Tremblay derisive names, among them *éminence rouge* ("red eminence") for Richelieu, in accordance with his red robe, and *éminence grise* ("gray eminence") for Père Joseph, owing to his gray Capuchin habit. The word *éminence*—from the Latin *eminentia*—was then used as an honorific title for cardinals. Richelieu's and Père Joseph's opponents, one may be assured, did not use the designation out of respect.

The expression *éminence grise* didn't make its way into English until the 1920s, when society felt the need for a word to define a private advisor with great (but clandestine) influence and power. Its original meaning, however, has been broadened over time to include any senior statesman or doyen, based on the erroneous assumption that "gray" referred to gray hair, supposedly an infallible indication of great maturity and wisdom. Little did Louis XIII's court know that their mockery would later become a rather respectable title.

Françoise Blanchard *and* Jeremy Leven

Entourage

[on too *rahj*]

From the verb *entourer* ("to surround"), which itself originates from the noun *entours* ("surroundings"), *entourage* was first recorded in the fifteenth century to describe the circle of friends, followers, or attendants who "surrounded" a particularly important person. The word is also used, on fewer occasions, as a synonym for surroundings and the environment.

The French sometimes use it to designate the ornaments decorating various objects, and, in fact, most personal *entourages* tend to be primarily ornamental.

Et voilà!

[ey vwa *lah*]

So simple and yet so difficult to translate, the expression *et voilà* most often translates as "and here you are" or "and there you go," and is used by the French on numerous occasions. The origins of *voilà* are the French verb *voir* ("to see") and the preposition *là* ("there"). The phrase *vois là* ("look there") was eventually contracted into *voilà*, a very handy word that applies to practically anyone or anything.

A simple sentence such as "Here they

come" becomes even simpler in French, with the phrase *Les voilà*. The reason the English would borrow such a trivial phrase probably has to do with the fact that, while English-speakers do have "So there you are," it has neither the ring nor efficiency of a well-delivered *Et voilà*.

Exposé

[ex po *zay*]

From the French verb *exposer* ("to exhibit") and the Latin *exponere*, *exposé* has been used in both French and English as a synonym for public statement or narration. As a verb, the expression multiplies its meanings and usage.

Exposing oneself may indicate either uncovering one's body and taking the risk of being subject to uncontrollable elements such as cold, heat, and danger, or of baring one's soul and being vulnerable to ridicule.

However, while French students work on their *exposé* assignments, the English press might publish *exposés* of unfavorable facts about a certain individual or institution. The difference between the French and English definitions lies in the intention of those revealing something that might otherwise be concealed from the public. The French, for example, make considerably less of a woman showing her breasts in public than do the English, who have extensive press coverage of such an *exposé*.

Faux pas

[foe *pa* / *foe* pa]

From the word *faux* ("false"), which finds its roots in the Latin *falsus,* and *pas* ("step"), this expression describes an embarrassing mistake or a diplomatically tactless remark or act. Among its synonyms are "blunder," "indiscretion," and *"gaffe,"* another French word that inspired comic-book author André Franquin, who named his now illustrious character Gaston Lagaffe after it. (Imagine, if you will, a lazy loser named Billy Blunder with a cat, a mouse, and a seagull as pets, and you'll get an idea of the laughable—and loveable—Gaston.)

There are quite a number of *faux*-words in French, such as *faux-semblant* ("pretense"), *faux-col* ("detachable collar"), *faux-fuyant* ("subterfuge"), *faux-monnayeur* ("counterfeiter"), *faux-naïf* ("disingenuous"), and *faux-ami* (literally "false friend"), a linguistic term that denounces the deceptive cognates between two languages. There are many examples, but, to name a few vocabulary *faux-amis: sympathie* in French is not "sympathy" but "friendliness"; *évidemment* is not "evidently" but "obviously"; *sensible,* not "sensible" but "sensitive"; *gentil,* not "gentle" but "kind"; and so on. Despite all these fakes, a French *faux-filet* is, in fact, real steak. There is absolutely no explanation for this.

Françoise Blanchard *and* Jeremy Leven

Femme fatale

[fem fa*tal* / fom fa*tal*]

A *femme fatale* is a dangerous woman, even more dangerous if you happen to be romantically involved with her. Though she is not necessarily a fatal woman à la Raymond Chandler, this is always a distinct possibility. Once considered the norm among French male-female relationships, sadly the combination of the women's liberation movement and improved shopping has seriously diminished the population in France of women whose only *raison d'être* (see entry on page 93) is to give their men a difficult time, prior to tossing them aside.

Reinforcing this is a somewhat different meaning in France, where a *femme fatale* is first and foremost an irresistible woman, leading one to wonder whether Frenchmen care less about the consequences if the liaison is sufficiently rewarding,

While the derivation of the word is a little hazy, André Maurois (1885–1967) has declared the perfect woman to be *"à la fois femme fatale et amazone, épouse irréprochable et maitresse adorée"* ("simultaneously femme fatale and amazon, irreproachable wife and adored mistress").

There is no record of an *homme fatal* in France, although a number of politicians, both recently and in the past, have aspired to that sobriquet. Still, a major defining characteristic of certain Frenchmen oftentimes seems to be the search for Maurois's perfect woman, and, where certain features are lacking, the expenditure of great amounts of energy to develop them.

Françoise Blanchard *and* Jeremy Leven

Film noir

[film nwar]

Literally translated as "black (or dark) film," the term was first coined in the 1950s by the movie critics of *Les Cahiers du Cinéma,* a French magazine dedicated to the art of filmmaking, of which François Truffaut, not yet a director, was one of the editors. The emergence of the *film noir* genre took place in the historical context of World War II, and is best characterized by the American cinema of the 1940s and 1950s. Hollywood then produced many dark and realistic dramas with plots often involving crime or intrigue. The main characters of a *film noir* are typically ambiguous and tormented, and their particular afflictions contribute to creating the distinctive gloomy atmosphere of this peculiar genre.

Film noir authors were essentially inspired by *romans noirs* ("dark novels"), which derived from mystery novels. No stranger to the bright hues of Impressionism, the French have gone on to identify *films roses* ("pink films") and *romans roses* ("pink novels"), *rose* being, of course, the color of flesh.

Franglais

[fron *glay*]

Franglais is a *portmanteau* made of two words: *français* (the French language) and *anglais* (the

English language). René Etiemble (1909–2002) came up with this term in 1964, when he published a book entitled *Parlez-vous franglais?* ("Do You Speak Franglais?"), in which he points a finger at the invasion of the French language by Anglo-Saxon neologisms (numbering in the thousands so far), as well as the copying of English expressions translated literally into French (*Ce n'est pas ma tasse de thé* for "It is not my cup of tea"). Among the most common borrowings from English that have long been absorbed by French dictionaries are *week-end, barbecue, football* (which throughout Europe is, of course, soccer), *jeans, hamburger* (including *le big-mac!*), *chewing-gum, gadget, living* (for living room), and many more.

This tendency to borrow English terms has gone up dramatically in the last decade, with the advent of the Internet, computers, and new technologies. But French scholars, aware of the potential problem, have been working hard to come up with new terms to counter the prolif- eration of Anglicisms that might dilute the purity of the French language. One of their proudest achievements is the 1970 pure-bred Latin word *logiciel,* the French term for "soft- ware." *Point locateur* has, fortunately, given way to *souris,* the French word for "mouse." As for the term "e-mail," the Academy, thankfully, has recently voted against the long and pompous *courrier électronique* and, instead, has embraced the Quebecois term *courriel,* made up of the word *courrier* ("correspondence") and the sylla- ble *él* (from *électronique*). In fact, the adoption of a Quebecois word by the purist French is a rarity that deserves to be noted. Finally, the word *baladeur* met a limited success before being, by public outcry, abandoned in favor of the word *Walkman*.

There is no doubt that the French have their hands full preserving the glory of their mother tongue, since French is the official language of the Olympics and the language of diplomacy, and is spoken in parts of Belgium, Switzerland, Canada, Louisiana, the Antilles, and Guyana, as well as being the official language in fifteen African countries. These many varieties of French might seem to make it difficult to determine a pure French language, but the French have solved this problem by appointing to the prestigious *Académie Française* guardian-scholars to protect the mother tongue from corruption. Their wisdom is doubted only by the general French populace, for whom using "Frenglish" (*franglais* in English) in everyday conversation has always seemed a very cool (also *cool* in French) thing to do. There is a suspicion that no matter how strongly French purists try imposing the *bon usage* of French language, it is bound to evolve, as it has for centuries.

Gauche / gaucherie

[gōsh / gōsh uh *ree*]

The origin of *gauche* possibly lies in the verb *gauchir* ("to bend," "to deform," or "to distort"), which comes from the Old French *guenchir* ("to make diversions"). It was long believed that left-handers, called *gauchers* in French, suffered from an unfortunate abnormality. The fact that *gauche* has been used to describe a socially clumsy action, conduct, or remark lacking tact and grace certainly didn't help their cause.

The word arrived into English during the mid-nineteenth century with its French meaning, and has since been employed as a synonym for "unpolished," when talking about a style or technique. From *gauche* naturally derived *gaucherie*, first recorded in French in the eighteenth century. The term, referring to awkward behavior or a blunder that betrays one's maladroitness, also included the sense of timidity.

We will leave it to the reader to explore which nationalities, when visiting Paris, for example, are seen by the good citizens of France to behave in a manner consistently *gauche*, being insufferably loud and poorly mannered, a deficiency attributed almost entirely to their tragic misfortune of not being French.

Guillotine

[*gill* luh teen / *gee* yo teen]

Despite its name, the beheading device called a *guillotine* was not invented by Doctor Joseph Ignace Guillotin (1738–1814), who was merely a supporter of a standard killing method that could be applied to all those sentenced to die, regardless of their social status or the nature of the charges against them. Monsieur Guillotin suggested decapitation as the appropriate choice for carrying out the death penalty, feeling it to be both exceptionally efficient and, presumably, an entirely painless way to die, although there is, obviously, a serious lack of anecdotal evidence to support the latter.

In point of fact, it was Doctor Antoine Louis (1723–1792), of the Academy of Medical

Studies, who was called upon to implement this merciful decision and who came up with the actual device, an improved version of the Italian *mannaja*. Indeed, the use of similar instruments had been widespread for the previous two centuries throughout Italy and Scotland, where the death machine was called "the maiden."

The *guillotine* consisted of a sharp blade gliding between two upright pieces of timber, first raised by a rope and then dropped on the neck of the victim below. It was originally nicknamed *Louison* or *Petite Louisette*, after its inventor, but it wasn't long before newspapers gave it the new title of *Madame Guillotine*, which came to be simply *guillotine*. Louis XVI, who was a skillful metalworker, supposedly gave a few nifty suggestions on improving its operation, clearly not expecting to experience its virtues firsthand. During the Great Terror that succeeded the French Revolution (1793–1794), the "widow" (as the crowd came to call it) killed more than 20,000 people. While the victims of the *guillotine* died quickly, old habits die slowly, and the last execution by *guillotine* was in 1977!

Ingenue

[*an* zha noo]

The Latin *ingenuus* carried the significance of "born free." In order to acquire the title of citizen of the Roman Republic, one had to prove that he was *ingenuus*, in other words, that he hadn't been born into slavery, or of a slave parent. Under the Roman Empire, the number of freed slaves grew tremendously. It then became even harder to become a citizen, for one had to prove that neither parents nor grandparents had been *libertines* (from the Latin *libertinus,* meaning "freed").

Time passed and *ingénue* took on its contemporary meaning of a naïve, artless, innocent, unsophisticated person, before arriving into English in the mid-nineteenth century. The word is usually applied to girls and young ladies, or to an actor playing the primary young female role.

From the close Latin root *ingeniosus* sprang another word, *ingénieux,* a French adjective that translates as "clever," a trait clearly not found in the two contestants on *Loft Story* (the French equivalent of the *Big Brother* TV show) whose now-infamous debate, seen in 2002 on French TV, focused on attempting to decipher the meaning of the word *ingénue,* convinced that it absolutely had to be, in some way, the feminine term for "genius." *Et voilà!*

Insouciant

[in *soo* see ant / an soo see *on*]

From the verb *soucier* ("to worry"), an *insouciant* is a person who literally doesn't worry. Used as a synonym for nonchalant or casual, *insouciant* describes someone unconcerned by the gravity of a matter or situation. The word *insouciance*, which has the same origin as *insouciant*, was adopted by the English in the late eighteenth century and translates as "indifference," "unconcern," and "carelessness."

In contrast to America's intense preoccupation with the dalliance of a recent president with a young intern, which occupied the media and the population for months on end, *insouciance* is an essential French trait and applies to public nudity (especially on giant posters in the metro stations), kissing in public (often of long duration), mistresses (especially if you are a politician), wines costing several years' income, and restaurant dishes served on fire.

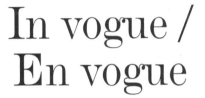

In vogue /
En vogue

[in vogh / anh vogh]

A word now immortalized by Madonna, the Queen of Pop, *vogue* is a French term from the fifteenth century that originated from the verb *voguer* ("to sail"), and possibly from the Italian *vogare* ("to row"). Its root goes back to the Indo-European term *wegh* ("to transport in a vehicle"), which is also the root of words such as *weight, way,* and so on. The imagery of a boat sailing on an unpredictable sea has led us to the fluctuations of fashion, with its ebbs and flows. In fact, the French word for "wave" is *vague,* closely resembling *vogue* in both spelling and etymology. *En vogue* translates as "in vogue" in English, meaning "in style" or "currently popular."

Surfing the waves of popularity is a thrilling but precarious sport, as many artists have experienced to their advantage or detriment. But while the sea is forgiving, the public is quite intransigent. Once one has acquired the favor of the population, the challenge is to keep it going. Yet the essence of a wave is to follow the invariable cycles dictated by the moon. As the tide goes, so goes fashion, coming and going in cycles, as it's been doing for years. What happened to pedal pushers and bell-bottoms? Nothing at all. They're back. For now.

Joie de vivre

[zhwa duh *vee* vr]

From the word *joie* ("joy") and the verb *vivre* ("to live"), this phrase literally translates as "joy of living" and is used to express enthusiasm and enjoyment of life, more than mere contentment. A person blessed with an infallible *joie de vivre* is in high spirits all the time, which, ultimately, brings happiness to his *entourage.*

Beware: *Mal de vivre* (literally "sickness of living") also exists in French, and applies to those in a more or less permanent state of depression and anxiety about life in general. Not a nation to do things halfway, the French are also responsible for the phrase *mal du siècle* ("century blues"), in which individual depression is extended to the entire world, the pleasures of fine wine, well-aged cheese, and excellent women lost to everyone.

Limousine

[*lim* oh zine / lee moo *zine*]

The shepherds of the Limousin province, to protect themselves from the elements, used to wear a heavy, hooded cloak called a *limousine,* which they brought along with them when they headed to Paris to find work in the nineteenth century. The first car to inherit the name was a six-seat vehicle in which the driver was—for the first time—protected from the rain by a hood and window. Previously, all motorized cars had been designed and manufactured according to the same pattern as *fiacres* (horse-drawn carriages), in which the driver was seated outside, controlling the horses, separated from the passengers in the coach. *Limousine* chauffeurs had no need to wear long coats, for their vehicles were now provided with hoods overhead.

In the early twentieth century, the *limousine*—also known as a limo—took on its current meaning of luxurious and spacious automobile driven by a chauffeur. Of course, the Americans and British have now done the French one better by upgrading the concept, inventing the stretch *limousine,* something which must seem quite curious to the traditionally small shepherds of Limousin.

Françoise Blanchard *and* Jeremy Leven

Lingerie

[lon zhuh *ray* / *lan* zhuh ree]

From the Latin *linum, linge* has been used as a French word since the thirteenth century to designate any items made out of linen, and applied to both clothing and household fabrics such as sheets. The word *lingerie* came along about a century later and referred to the manufacturing and trading of linen objects. That definition was soon replaced by another, as a *lingerie* became the room or space (within a community or any habitation) dedicated to the washing and ironing of linens.

These definitions have since become obsolete, and the modern meaning of *lingerie* in both languages (although the final syllable is pronounced "ee" in French and "ay" in

English), is now applied exclusively to women's nightclothes and fine quality undergarments. It appears that some English-speaking visionary in the women's apparel industry reached the conclusion that to sell women's sexy undergarments he stood a far greater chance of success if he turned to the great repository of female sexuality, France, and called his silk and lace items *lingerie* rather than underwear. Dissatisfied that the French word didn't sound French enough, and familiar with words such

as *café* and *risqué*, he Frenched it up by pro-
nouncing it lon-zhuh-*ray*. At first baffled by
wealthy Frenchwomen returning from abroad
and asking for sexy *lingerie* (sheets, napkins,
and tablecloths) to seduce their husbands and
lovers, the French tradesmen quickly caught
on and began selling women *lingerie* instead of
underwear (*sous-vêtements*), but were under-
standably resistant to changing the pronunciation of their word.

Ménage à trois

[may *najh* ah trwa]

From the French *ménage,* meaning both "house-hold" and "housecleaning," and *à trois,* meaning "with three people," *ménage à trois* translates as a household of three, customarily sharing more than just the same roof and domestic tasks. Indeed, sex is definitely part of the deal: the expression *ménage à trois* does not necessarily indicate a threesome, but it definitely implies that at least one member of the household is sexually involved with both of the others.

The practicality of such a concept may not be obvious to those who are unfamiliar with it, but the idea of having two men bringing home the bacon or two women sharing the cooking and the cleaning (among other things) certainly seems appealing. The definition of a *ménage à trois* is not specific regarding the genders of the three people involved in this love triangle, so many variations are yours for the taking. In Paris, where apartments are scarce, finding a *ménage* of an adequate size can often be more of a problem than finding the *trois*.

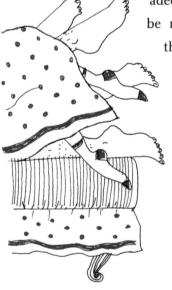

Moustache

[*mus* tash / moose *tash*]

Back in the fifteenth century, the French acquired this word from the Italian *mostaccio,* which itself derived from the Greek *mustaki* and the Old Greek *mustax,* used to describe the upper lip. The word voyaged to Italy via Venice before entering France thanks to the campaign of Charles VIII.

Also spelled *mustache* in English, *moustache* is now used in reference to the beard (and sometimes to the milk) that appears above the lips. For a long time, men have put a great deal of thought and care into the maintenance of their *moustaches,* following strict rules set by fashion trends, which demanded that the hairy ornament be either curled, trimmed, bushy, or shaved, depending on the epoch. Once Clemenceau left us, the trend largely disappeared in France.

Naïf, naïve

[nah *eef,* nah *eve*]

From the Latin *nativus* ("native"), the noun or adjective *naïf* (and its feminine form, *naïve,* used only as an adjective) comes from the verb *naître* ("to be born"), leading logically to the concept of being as innocent as a newborn. While the Romans would call uneducated peasants by this name, we prefer to employ it as a reproach for one's lack of maturity or awareness, a trait typically found among inappropriately confident youngsters without entirely excluding their unrealistic elders.

It has been used with its modern meaning of "innocence" in both French and English since the sixteenth century. During the twentieth century there appeared a new variety of *naïf*: *faux-naïf*, describing one whose apparent innocence is but a false show, the challenge now being to distinguish the genuine *naïf* from the deceptive one, not always an easy task.

Negligee

[*neh* glee zhay]

From the Latin *negligere*, *negligee* or *negligé* (originally written *négligée* in French) is the feminine adjectival form of *négliger,* a French verb first recorded in the early fourteenth century and meaning "to neglect." The word arrived into English in the mid-eighteenth century with quite a different definition. Indeed, it was (and still is) used to describe a woman's thin dressing gown, as well as her informal attire. The French may also use it to describe one's appearance as being "neglected," a curious secondary meaning as, on both sides of the Atlantic, men tend not to neglect a woman appearing before them in a *negligee.*

Nouveau riche

[noo voh *reesh*]

A *nouveau riche*, or *parvenu*, is a person who has recently risen to wealth without acquiring the manners and good taste of the class to which he now belongs, thus bringing about the disapproving judgment of the legitimate members of high society. This expression kept its French meaning when it arrived in English at the beginning of the nineteenth century.

Among today's crowd of yuppies and bobos (*bourgeois-bohêmes*), the *nouveau riche* has become harder to spot. Some recent unfortunate events of an economic nature have turned the *nouveau riche* into an endangered species. Not to fret, the stock market's downfall has now provided society with the emergence of a new species: the *nouveau pauvre* (newly impoverished), who, like his newly enriched counterpart, is shunned by society. Although this French expression hasn't yet made its way into English, we suspect it is merely a matter of time.

Panache

[pa *nash* / pa *nosh*]

In French and English since the 1500s, *panache* originally comes from the Italian *pennacchio* ("tuft of feathers"), which itself comes from the Latin *penna*, "feather." In ancient times, the dash of those blessed with a certain *panache* was emphasized by a colorful plume worn as an ornament on a knight's helmet or a nobleman's hat. Today, in both French and English, the word is used figuratively to describe behavior with special flamboyance and pizzazz, often accompanied by a certain elegance. The French are especially adept at this, while the English claim to have improved upon the French version. In any event, acting with *panache* has become a feather in both their caps.

The illustrious French King Henry IV (1553–1610) is known to have shouted to his men in the midst of a chaotic battle against the Catholic army at Ivry, on March 14, 1590: *"Voici votre roi! . . . Si vos cornettes vous manquent, ralliez-vous à mon panache blanc, vous le trouverez au chemin de la victoire et de l'honneur!"* ("Here is your king! If your cornets fail, rally behind my white panache, and you will find the road to victory and honor!") It is likely the white

feather was easy to spot, but the king's magnif-
icence and heroism certainly radiated far more
panache than any ornament, and doubtless
earned him the victory that day. History has
not yet determined whether he could have displayed the same *panache* without the *plume*.

Pièce de résistance

[pee ess duh ray zeess *tonce*]

Composed of the three words *pièce* ("piece"), *de*
("of"), and *résistance* ("strength" or "solidity"), a
pièce de résistance often refers to the main
course of a meal, consisting of a substantial

and frequently flamboyant dish. By extension, the expression has come to apply to any notable event or piece in a program, collection, or series, remarkable by its special importance and grandness, though not necessarily suitable for eating. While it may be impossible to "resist" a *pièce de résistance,* it has no relation to the kind of resistance found in *La Résistance,* an underground movement against the German occupation of France during World War II, seen by many as the *pièce de résistance* of a proud France.

Françoise Blanchard *and* Jeremy Leven

Pied-à-terre

[pee ay dah *tare* / pee ay ah *tare*]

Literally translated as "foot-to-ground," this expression was originally a trumpet call that ordered the horsemen or cavalrymen to get off their horses and rest momentarily. It naturally evolved after the eighteenth century into a synonym for a temporary residence or part-time lodging, usually meant for travelers who, after a long journey, were in need of a place to rest. The word was adopted by the English soon afterward, with the same meaning.

After relocating to the suburbs during the last century, we are now witnessing something of a reversal, as baby boomers with empty nests are returning to the city, and, while maintaining their suburban residences, are purchasing *pieds-à-terre* in town for occasional stays, as a way to preserve a foothold in the city. This is not a new phenomenon, as, not so long ago, yuppie dot-com millionaires made quite a thing about purchasing elaborate *pieds-à-terre*, only to find themselves, in due time, having to get off their high horses.

Protégé

[*pro* tuh zhay / pro teh *zhay*]

In French since the mid-eighteenth century, *protégé*, from the verb *protéger* ("to protect") and the Latin *protegere*, can be used both as a noun and as an adjective. The English adopted the noun form in the late eighteenth century, using *protégé* and its feminine, *protégée,* to refer to someone under the protective wing or chaperonage of an influential person, usually a benefactor interested in developing his/her pupil's career by providing support as well as protection.

The French have developed an analogy between a protector-*protégé* relationship and that of a horse trainer and his/her charges. Thus, the promising youngster is often called a *poulain* ("foal"), and the successful school or training facility an *écurie* ("stable"). In French, these words still apply to animals and stables, but, one assumes, with a lesser degree of ambition for their careers and less gloating by their trainers.

Raison d'être

[ray zon *detr*]

Literally "reason to be," *raison d'être* is an expression used by both the French and English since the mid-nineteenth century to denote the purpose of a person's or a thing's existence, as in the phrase *"être ou ne pas être"* ("to be or not to be"), the words that launched Hamlet's search for his own personal *raison d'être*.

Françoise Blanchard *and* Jeremy Leven

Recherché

[ruh share *shay*]

The verb *rechercher* ("to search" or "to look for") is the origin of this adjective, used in French since the late sixteenth century to define something that is carefully thought out and studied, and by extension refined, elegant, and exquisite. The word may also occasionally be used as a synonym for "rare," "unusual," and even "far-fetched," but more often its similarity to *chic* prevails. Judging from the ubiquitous signs in New York City that label small stores, coffee shops, and bakeries as *boutiques, cafés, bistros,* and *pâtisseries,* to become *recherché* may require nothing more than the simple translation of a name from English to French.

Rendezvous

[*ron* day voo]

Se rendre ("to surrender oneself") is the original verb upon which this expression is based. In its conjugated form, *rendez-vous* means "Give yourself up," a cry heard in the mouths of soldiers addressing the enemy or policemen arresting criminals. The verb is also used within a formal sentence when asking someone to go to a specific location. Later on, the conjugated form of the original verb turned into an expression now commonly used in both French and English when identifying an appointment, or the place and time of a meeting.

Depending on the context, *rendezvous* will refer to a specific location where a crowd usually gathers, the headquarters of a gang, or even an appointed place to gather army troops or fleets.

The French also apply the expression to the actual person one is meeting, resulting in such phrases as "Your rendez-vous has arrived." While the English often use it as a synonym for a romantic encounter, the French are more precise and call such a meeting a *rendez-vous galant* ("romantic *rendezvous*"). To keep up with the times, the French now have the *rendez-vous spatial* ("space *rendezvous*"), a meeting of two or more craft in outer space, while the more efficient and down-to-earth Americans have now broken new ground in personal encounters by pioneering, for those seeking mates and having exceptional memories, the eight-minute informational amorous *rendezvous* marathon.

Repartee

[rep ar *tee* / rep ar *tay*]

First recorded in French in the early seventeenth century, the expression comes from the verb *repartir* ("to go again"), and is actually written *repartie* in French. The meaning, however, is the same in both languages and describes a spontaneous and witty comment that hits the spot after it has bounced back on a previous argument. In English, *repartee* may also be used as a synonym for *riposte* (another French word), indicating a clever and adroit retort.

For centuries, the French have cultivated the art of fencing with both swords and words, persuaded that ridicule is as deadly a weapon as any blade. At one time, the art of displaying one's skills in *repartee* seemed to be the only way to avoid dying from raillery in court. But times have changed, and today we are far more inclined to applaud the not very subtle art of

self-derision over the witty answer. As French writer Boris Vian (1920–1959) once wrote: *"Le ridicule ne tue plus, nulle part, mais aux U.S.A. il enrichit drôlement."* ("Ridicule doesn't kill anymore, anywhere, but in America, it enriches quite a bit.")

Résumé

[*rez* uh may / *ray* zoo *may*]

A perfect example of a *faux-ami* (see *faux pas* for further information), *résumé* comes from the verb *résumer* ("to summarize" or "to sum up") and the Latin *resumere,* and has been used by the French since the mid-eighteenth century when referring to a shortened version of a text, with synonyms such as "abstract," "epitome," and "recapitulation." Although the English retained this original meaning, they added a new definition to the word, now mostly used in reference to the brief statement of one's educational background and professional experiences, known as *curriculum vitae* by the French (who often shorten it to CV).

Apart from its appellation, there are quite a few differences between a French and an American *résumé,* such as the inclusion of a photograph of oneself, almost always obligatory in a French CV, along with the date and place of birth, the marital status, and the mention of a driver's license (when applicable). An English *résumé* will omit this information in order to avoid having the hiring process biased by what may be considered discriminatory data regarding age, race, sexual orientation, and even, depending on the individual and the quality of the photo, physical attractiveness. Rest assured, however, that French legislation also protects employees against discriminatory hiring practices, assuming they can be proven. However, there is no reason for alarm. With an unemployment rate frequently near 10 percent, employers having to pay nearly 70 percent in additional fringes while giving their employees what amounts to an obligatory two months a year off, along with severe restrictions on firing an employee, French employers are not exactly grabbing for *résumés*.

Risqué

[ris *kay*]

Risqué is the past participle of the verb *risquer,* meaning "to risk." While the French use *risqué* as an adjective to describe a potentially dangerous situation (as in "risky"), the English have been using it since the mid-nineteenth century in reference to daring or inappropriate lyrics, comments, stories, films, and so on, suggestive of sexual indecency.

While the French word has no sexual connotation whatsoever since, apparently, the French see little risk in being *risqué*, one can only wonder what dangers the English saw looming ahead, and what career Tom Cruise might have launched had he starred in a film entitled *Risqué Business*.

Roman
à clef

[row *mon* ah *clay*]

Also written *roman à clé* in French, this three-hundred-year-old expression translates literally as a novel with a key. Such a book tells the story of recent events, disguised as fiction, in which the identities of the main characters are concealed. A list giving the "key" to match the real names with the aliases was often published after the book's release. Among the numerous existing "key" novels are *Point Counter Point* by Aldous Huxley, which portrays D. H. Lawrence and other prominent figures of his time; *The Blithedale Romance* by Nathaniel Hawthorne; about Herman Melville; and

Samaritan by Philippe van Rijndt, featuring Pope John Paul II.

In poetry, authors also used a method called *acrostiche* in French to hide secret messages within their poems. Messages were conveyed surreptitiously by using the first letter or word of each line. The reader is referred to the poem written by Alfred de Musset (1810–1857) to George Sand (1804–1876), in which he secretly yet bluntly asks when he may sleep with her. The following two verses are her alleged answer:

"Cette insigne faveur que votre coeur réclame /
Nuit à ma renommée et répugne à mon âme." ("This remarkable favor that your heart demands / Threatens my reputation and repulses my soul.")

The first words of each line are *cette* and *nuit*: tonight.

R.S.V.P.

R.S.V.P. is merely the abbreviation of *Répondez s'il vous plaît*, meaning "Answer, please," a phrase often found at the bottom of a formal invitation, requesting the invitee to make his decision known, usually before a specified deadline. The S.V.P. abbreviation is often used by the French, whose equivalent of "please" is regrettably long, as it actually means "if you

please." As for the added "V" of R.V.S.V.P., it stands for the adverb *vite* ("quickly"), when an answer is requested promptly. Now aware of its meaning, one will know not to write "R.S.V.P. please," an unforgivable pleonasm.

For those interested in minutiae, R.S.V.P. also stands for Resource reSerVation Protocol, as well as Revolutionary Surrealist Vandal Party.

Sangfroid

[sanh frwa]

Written *sang-froid* in French, the word is made of the noun *sang* ("blood") and the adjective *froid* ("cold"), and can be best translated as "cold blood," when talking about a crime, or as "calm" or "self-control" when referring to someone's attitude, especially when under pressure or facing a dangerous or emergency situation. In French since the seventeenth century, the word was borrowed by English a century later, with its original meaning of poise and composure.

By opposition, *sang chaud* refers to the temper of a hot-blooded person, an expression the English apparently felt no need to borrow.

Savoir faire

[sav wahr *fare*]

This expression is made of two separate French verbs, *savoir* ("to know") and *faire* ("to do"), thus creating an expression translated as "to know how to do," and which specifically applies to someone's tact and knowledge of social behavior. In French since the late seventeenth century, *savoir-faire* was borrowed by the English in the early nineteenth century and further applied to specific know-how, in terms of expertise, experience, knowledge, and techniques accumulated by an individual or company. But no sooner did the French adopt this new meaning from abroad than the English dropped it and retained only the definition of "smooth social skill."

Another French expression, *savoir-vivre* ("to know how to live"), made its way into English, being defined as "good manners" and "etiquette," identical to the French meaning. There is no record of any individual, either French or English, identified as simultaneously being blessed with *savoir faire* and *savoir-vivre.*

Soirée

[swa *ray*]

The French had been using *soirée* nearly three hundred years before the English first borrowed the word in the early nineteenth century. Originating from the Latin *serus* ("late"), which gave the French *soir* ("evening"), *soirée* refers precisely to the time between the sun's setting and our falling asleep. The second—and more modern—meaning of *soirée* is a social gathering or reception held in the evening, usually at a home.

By extension, the French apply *soirée* to the evening performance of a show (as opposed to the *matinée*), as well as using it as an adjective to describe the formal gown—*de rigueur* for attending such an event—otherwise known as an evening gown.

Soupçon

[soop *sohn*]

The word *soupçon* crossed over to English in the mid-eighteenth century as a synonym for "trace," "hint," or "touch," referring to a slight but distinct quality. The Latin *suspicio* gave the French language *sospeçon,* which became, in the mid-1500s, the *soupçon* we know today. The word is used in French to describe suspicion toward someone whose intentions seem questionable. The French also use it when noticing a clue that hints at the presence of something that exists in a very small amount, whether it be a flavor, a color, or a feeling.

Oftentimes, a *soupçon* is barely traceable, especially in France, where everything (above all food and humor) is all about subtlety and nuance.

Souvenir

[soo veh *near*]

This oft-used word comes from the Latin *sub-venire* ("to come to mind"), from which sprang the Old French word *suvenir,* which later became the verb *se souvenir* ("to remember"). It was not until the fourteenth century that the verb turned into a noun, with meanings such as "memory," "recollection," "reminiscence," and "memorabilia." It was with this last definition that the word was introduced into English, as a synonym for "keepsake," or any item with sentimental value attached to it.

Today it is also applied to trinkets sold in gift shops in tourist areas. These items, often made in Asia and sold by the thousands, are far from being unique relics. Yet their status as *souvenirs* makes them a must-buy for any tourist whose friends and relatives are expecting "a little something" from that trip abroad. The

decline of the word from "something of great sentimental value" to "a little something" is sad indeed, especially considering how quickly these mementos find their way into the trash. One can only wonder about the short-term *souvenirs* (memories) of those purchasing *souvenirs*.

Suave

[swav / soo *ahv*]

The adjective *suave* originated from the Latin *suavis* ("soft") and entered both the French and English vocabularies in the late fifteenth century to designate the sweet, delicious, pleasant, and exquisite qualities of an individual or object. The adjective often applies to fragrances and flavors, and is now primarily suggestive of courtesy, refinement, and sophistication when talking about someone's manner or speech. Among *suave*'s most common synonyms are "urbane" and "smooth."

From *suave* derived several words such as "suavely," "suaveness," and "suavity," possibly all created to reflect the extreme and sometimes even superficial smoothness that some feel is so typically British—in the manner of James Bond—and others feel is descriptive of every Frenchman.

Tête-à-tête

[tet ah tet]

Tête is the French word for "head," which came from the medieval Latin *testa* ("skull" or "cranium"). The expression *tête-à-tête* literally means "head-to-head" and is a visual reference to the position of two people in the middle of a private talk, facing each other. Thus the expression has been used to describe a situation in which two people isolate themselves to talk, usually in close proximity. When the expression arrived in English in the late seventeenth century, it took on the original meaning of a private conversation, along with adjectival and adverbial uses to signify, respectively, "confidential" and "face-to-face."

Around 1780, the French named a small

couch a *tête-à-tête*. It was fashioned to seat only two people, forcing them into a *tête-à-tête*, and by 1900 the set of dishware designed to serve breakfast for two was also identified as a *tête-à-tête*. Never lacking inspiration for visual imagery, the French came up with another expression, *tête-a-queue* (literally "head-to-tail"), mostly employed with regard to the sudden movement of a horse turning around, as well as the abrupt spinning of a vehicle moving backward—if into another vehicle, often resulting in a rather heated *tête-à-tête*.

Tour de force

[toor duh *forss*]

The French *tour* has many meanings, among them "trick" (as in a magic trick, *tour de magie*). The expression thus literally translates as "trick of strength," commonly known as a "feat of strength" in English. The French first used it to mean an exercise that required a great deal of sustained strength. Later on, the expression applied to any exploit or performance accomplished skillfully and with ingenuity.

Once the expression became part of the English language, in the early nineteenth century, it referred to extraordinary artistic, sports, or literary performances, along with other impressive deeds. The expression becomes especially meaningful when the achiever has faced and overcome unfavorable circumstances, in which case the *tour de force* takes the audience by surprise, suggesting a *tour de magie.*

Triage

[tree *azh* or *tree* azh]

Used by the French since 1317 to describe the act of sorting, *triage* comes from the verb *trier* ("to sort") and was first employed in English in the early twentieth century. However, its meaning became slightly more specific, as it applied only to the sorting of wounded soldiers or victims of accidents in order to determine who deserved priority treatment. Such a practice allowed for more survivors, as the critically injured were given attention more quickly. *Triage* later became a more generic term, and its definition evolved to include any assignment of priority done in response to a crisis. It is used both as an adjective and as a verb.

The French have expanded the original concept and now apply it to transportation (a *triage* station is where railroad cars are sorted to form trains), geology (when elements are naturally separated), and more generally, to any location where *triages* of items are performed. As ubiquitous as the usage has become, it is not surprising to find that, while young Frenchmen seem to be less concerned with classifying the women they meet at the local clubs, Frenchwomen seem to have developed a rather precise and acute system of *triage* in similar social circumstances.

Françoise Blanchard *and* Jeremy Leven

Trompe l'œil

[tromp *loy*]

From the verb *tromper* ("to deceive") and *œil* ("eye"), *trompe l'œil* refers to artwork that tricks the eye by its realistic appearance and its three-dimensional perspective, thus creating an optical illusion. Such technique is often used in interior decorating in order to add depth to a room, or texture to a wall, ceiling, or floor by imitating stones such as marble. The expression *trompe l'œil* may also be used to refer to anyone or anything which conveys the characteristics of a *trompe l'œil* painting in its misleading appearance. In French since the early 1800s, the word travelled to English by the end of the century as both noun and adjective.

A few decades after the expression's first

occurrence, the French came up with another kind of *trompe*, a *trompe-la-mort* (literally "deceiver of death"), in reference to someone whom death cannot seem to kill, no matter how ill he is or what injury he may encounter. While survival is usually a good thing, this may be an exception.

Vaudeville

[*vawd* vill / *voh* duh veel]

Before becoming the light and entertaining comedy acts and skits we know today, *vaudeville* meant satirical popular and drinking songs that were performed by minstrels and poet-singers beginning in the fifteenth century. The origin of the word is uncertain and debatable. Some sources assume that *vaudevilles* were originally named after Val-de-Vire, a village in Normandy, said to be the birthplace of Olivier Bassin, author of the first *vaudevilles*.

During the next century, however, another genre of *chansons*, songs celebrating courtly love, appeared. They were named *voix de ville* (literally "voices of the city"), probably after the city of Paris, where these songs were first heard. It is possible that the public amalgamated the two and created the term *vaudeville*, which has been used ever since to describe a variety show with ballet numbers, pantomimes, songs, and dialogues, traditionally performed at village fairs. A more recent hypothesis mentions the two Old French verbs *vauder* and *virer* (later altered into *ville*), both meaning "to turn" and "to spin," the idea being that the jolly songs were meant to make one "spin" the night away, quite an extension of logic.

By the eighteenth century, the genre

underwent a separation between the singing *vaudeville,* which turned into the *opéra comique* in 1743, and the *vaudeville* that favored dialogue, thus combining with the more satirical *burlesque* genre, often called farce. The nineteenth century was the golden age of *vaudevilles,* with celebrated authors such as Augustin Scribe (1791–1861), Eugène Labiche (1815–1888), George Courteline (1858–1929), and Georges Feydeau (1862–1921), whose plays are still performed today.

The contemporary French *vaudeville* has given way to the *comédie de boulevard,* a theatrical show tailored to entertain a popular crowd. In America, *vaudeville* virtually disappeared after the advent of talking pictures in 1927, unless, of course, one includes the popular entertainment of diversionary song and dance also known as "politics."

Françoise Blanchard *and* Jeremy Leven

Vignette

[veen *yet*]

Vignette (literally "small vine") is the diminutive of another French word, *vigne* ("vine"), which comes from the Latin word *vinum* ("wine") and has been in French since the thirteenth century. Originally, the *vignette* was a carved architectural decoration representing vine leaves. Today its definition includes decorative motifs on the front or last page of a book, letterhead designs (which may be a drawing or initials), ornamental drawings framing medieval miniature engravings and artworks, or illustrations within a book, newspaper, or even a comic book. In 1854 the sense of *vignette* expanded to brand logos and, in the early twentieth century, also included any kind of label attached to an item, usually as a method of identification.

The English felt the need to incorporate *vignette* into their vocabulary in the mid–eighteenth century but took the liberty of modifying the original definition. Thus, *vignette* came to mean a drawing or illustration gradually shaded in order not to be marked off by a lined border, or, in photography, a portrait from head to shoulders, also gradually shading into a darkened background. Used as a verb, *vignette* means "to soften the edges" (of a picture). Coincidentally, it may also be a synonym for a short literary sketch or account. In the entertainment

business, *vignette* is also employed when talking about a brief scene (whether in a movie or a play). With abundant definitions, *vignette* is one small leaf that has branched out into a forest— for the French, undeniable proof of the wonders of a good wine.

Voyeur

[voy *yur* / vwa *yur*]

Voyeur is derived from the verb *voir,* meaning "to see," and translates literally as "one who sees." In the early eighteenth century, the French used the word to identify a spectator, most often an individual who peered out of deviant curiosity while distancing himself from the affair. Since the end of the nineteenth century, the significance of the word has been the same in French and English, when the expression started to be used to describe a viewer who obtains sexual gratification from observing sexual or intimate acts, usually secretively.

Although the French deny it, the paternity of the word suggests that they are the inventors of voyeurism. Doubters might want to walk down a beach on the Riviera during the summer, where scores of amused topless French women dare men not to be *voyeurs*.

About the Authors

FRANÇOISE BLANCHARD is a well-travelled Frenchwoman who spent several years in the United States, where she met coauthor Jeremy Leven. After three years of collaboration, primarily on film projects, she returned home to Paris to write. She now lives in Seoul, Korea, with her husband, Jung-Soon Choi.

JEREMY LEVEN veered from a career in the field of neuropsychiatry to became a novelist, a screenwriter *(Creator, Playing for Keeps, The Legend of Bagger Vance, Crazy as Hell, Alex and Emma, The Notebook)*, and a director *(Don Juan Demarco,* which he also wrote). He divides his time among Paris, Connecticut, and New York City.